# THE PERIOD ROOMS OF RUTH McCHESNEY

## Anne Day Smith

KALMBACH BOOKS

Printed in the United States of America.

Design: Kristi Ludwig
Edited by: Sybil Sosin, Mary Algozin
Cover photo: Courtesy American Museum in Britain


Publisher's Cataloging in Publication
(Prepared by Quality Books Inc.)

Smith, Anne Day.
    The period rooms of Ruth McChesney /
Anne Day Smith.
        p.   cm.
        Includes index.
        ISBN 0-89024-301-8

    1.  Miniature rooms.   2.  Interior decoration.
3.  McChesney, Ruth—Art collections.   I.  Title.

NK2117.M54S65 1997          747'.0228
                            QBI96-40674

**Disclaimer**
We have tried to be as accurate as possible in the identification and attribution of the many individual items shown in this book. As in any collection, it is not always possible to identify every item, and we sincerely apologize for any errors or omissions.

Printed in the U.S.A. by Image Graphics, Paducah, KY

To "M. E."

*For her courage and our friendship*

# ABOUT THE AUTHOR

**A**nne Day Smith has been writing professionally since high school and specializing in miniatures since the late 1970s, when she began writing and taking photographs for *Nutshell News* as well as other magazines and newspapers. She has traveled extensively around the country, covering miniatures shows, interviewing artisans, and visiting miniatures collections.

She is the author of four previous books about miniatures: *Interior Design in Miniature*, published in 1986; *Masters in Miniature*, published in 1987; *The Andrews Collection: Personal Treasures*, published in 1988; and *Brooke Tucker's Golden Christmas: Building a Miniature Masterpiece,* published in 1996. She also contributed to *Treasures in Miniature*, published in 1993.

Anne is also an ardent collector of miniatures and still has the dollhouse she played with as a child. She and her husband, Gerry, a recently retired retail executive, have three grown sons and six grandchildren. They live in a restored eighteenth-century house in Dresden, Maine.

## RUTH McCHESNEY'S ROOMS IN MUSEUMS

**Breteuil:** The Carnegie Museum of Art, Pittsburgh, Pennsylvania

**Port Royal entrance hall; Jefferson hall and dining room:** The American Museum in Britain, Claverton Manor, Bath, England

**Covent Garden supper room; French Transitional room:** Campbell Art Gallery, Sewickley Academy, Sewickley, Pennsylvania

**Wilpen parlor:** Sewickley Valley Historical Society, Sewickley, Pennsylvania

**Cecil bedroom:** The Henry Francis duPont Winterthur Museum, Wilmington, Delaware

Ruth McChesney's rooms have also been shown in two of the leading magazines for miniatures enthusiasts:

*Nutshell News,* Kalmbach Publishing Co., P. O. Box 1612, Waukesha, WI 53187

*International Dolls House News,* Nexus Special Interests Ltd., Nexus House, Boundary Way, Hemel Hempstead, Herts HP2 7ST, England

# CONTENTS

# PROLOGUE

*Left to right: Tom, Ruth, and Bill McChesney.*

At the time of life when most people are thinking of retirement, our mother Ruth McChesney launched a new career in miniatures. Due to our closeness to her, we can see that she may have been inadvertently preparing for this work all her life.

Mother has always had a sense of style and color. She and our father shared a strong concern for education for everyone. Consistent with well-educated ladies of her generation, she focused her career on the home: us, her family, and a variety of civic responsibilities, including one remarkable achievement of being the driving force in the creation of the Donald Reed Speech Center in Westchester, New York. Some of her activities are described in this book's biography section. Mother knows how to get things done.

Our earliest memories revolve around the two houses Mother developed into homes for us in Sewickley. One, a period Victorian, had her researching in decorative arts publications and painstakingly pursuing the right antiques and finish for each room. We grew up there, but we were not oblivious to the style and comfort we enjoyed. Their next house, during our college years, was an exquisite copy of Bremo, a country house designed in Thomas Jefferson's style. It was a new challenge for her to adapt to a different style while maintaining a personal and warm sense of home. This house triggered an architectural investigation that both our parents enjoyed, and it is also the model for one of Mother's earliest rooms. We had the luck to see her varied interests develop into a remarkable attention to detail and a determination that led to the creation of

fascinating rooms, some of which we had the pleasure to have in our homes, and many of which are seen in this book.

With the progressive physical disability of our father after his retirement in 1970, Mother channeled her interests with her organizational skills and attention to detail into the creation of the many rooms presented here. Her direct involvement was the duplication in miniature of tapestries, carpets, and other fabrics in exacting detail, under a magnifying lamp, at 1600 stitches to the square inch. Achieving artisan status in the International Guild of Miniature Artisans when over seventy years old is an admirable accomplishment.

Entering this circle of miniature artisans provided inspiration and support for her new ideas and made it possible for her to conceive, design, participate in, and implement the creation of museum-quality rooms. Creating these rooms is an expression of her basic desire to educate, to inform. Perhaps because she was the daughter of an author, Mother wants to make a contribution, and her skill, talent, and niche is miniatures. Her rooms, in this book, in museums, in schools, will educate viewers about period lifestyles.

As brothers we have discovered interests in architecture and home remodeling and perhaps a sense of style because of our mother. As a family we all are fortunate to share artistic partnership with our mother as she energetically enters her eighties, and we look forward to sharing her next creation.

William S. McChesney, Jr.
Thomas B. McChesney

# INTRODUCTION

Like a magnet, it draws you in. Like a three-dimensional painting, it commands your attention. You become a part of this captivating scene as your eye takes in each tiny object, and you are mesmerized by the view before you. This fascinating object of your attention is a miniature room, a precisely controlled glimpse into a more perfect world.

Miniatures have been a part of our world since the earliest civilizations. The Egyptians believed that miniature objects in their tombs served in the after life in the same capacity as the full-sized originals had in this one. There were realistic miniature replicas even then. Much later, in the sixteenth century, miniature houses were built, usually for royal or wealthy families. Today those surviving structures, or their written inventories, serve as a faithful record, a social history of the period.

Ever since then, miniatures have been treasured and admired, and dollhouses have been built and lovingly cared for. And in the twentieth century two women, one in England and one in the United States, began to design and build exquisite miniature rooms, most of them still on public view today. Katherine Carlisle of London and Narcissa Thorne of Chicago never met and probably never even corresponded, but their work was quite similar. The two women worked at about the same time, and both had been entranced with all things miniature since childhood. During the time they were working, from about 1920 to 1940, period rooms in museums were both popular and numerous. That is no longer the case, and the scarcity of miniature period rooms may be one reason why these small works of art have enjoyed a renaissance in recent years.

Both Mrs. Carlisle and Mrs. Thorne are gone now, but their legacy lives on as others have continued their work. In this book we feature a well-known contemporary builder of period rooms in miniature: Ruth B. McChesney of Sewickley, Pennsylvania. There are many parallels in the work of the three women.

Like Mrs. Carlisle and Mrs. Thorne before her, Ruth McChesney personally coordinates each of her projects, beginning with extensive research. Like her predecessors, she commissions the work of some of the finest artisans producing miniatures today. She also combines appropriate antique miniatures with the contemporary work. Just as Mrs. Carlisle, who was a devoted needleworker, used her petit point creations in her rooms, Ruth displays examples of her own needlework in hers, often a handsome and historic carpet.

And like these earlier period rooms in miniature, Ruth's do not contain renderings of human figures. Instead, her trademark is to place an appropriate dog in each room. The rooms seem to come alive because of them.

A period room tells a story, and if done correctly, presents the viewer with a precise visual representation of the period. Like her predecessors, Ruth takes great pains to execute rooms that evoke the feeling of the period they represent. Often these miniature rooms are accurate, faithfully executed copies of the original rooms. Some illustrate particular aspects of the period. The attention to detail is astounding.

As you turn these pages, imagine a curtain rising in the theater as each setting draws you in, commands your attention, transports you visually into a more perfect world. It is both a very personal and a very special little world, as seen through the eyes of Ruth B. McChesney.

# 1
# CANDY HOUSES

*Large streams from little fountains flow,*
*Tall oaks from little acorns grow.*
*—David Everett (1770–1813)*

Years ago, when their two sons were young, Bill and Ruth McChesney began a family Christmas tradition of building and decorating a house with icing and candy. "Being a Scot," the younger Bill McChesney remembers, "my father made it out of wood so he could use it again." The plywood house sat on a breadboard, had glass windows, and was lighted.

Ruth recalls with delight making miniature furniture of chocolate and braiding rugs with long strings of licorice. "The difficulty was getting long candies in different colors to braid the rug," she reminisces. "I used to braid a very cute little black one to put by the front door." She also remembers using a Necco wafer for a clock face "and putting all the little numbers on it. It was really charming."

That first year, the McChesneys invited their adult neighbors to help decorate the candy house; in ensuing

*An early McChesney candy house. Photo courtesy Ruth McChesney.*

*Ice cream cones, paper towel rolls, and foam core are incorporated into the foundation of this candy structure, a famous French chateau called Chenonçeau, located on the Cher river. Photo courtesy Bill McChesney.*

years the guest list increased and included children. Ruth remembers collecting candy "for quite a few months," so as to have the assortment needed for shutters, the roof, and architectural details.

Sometimes the houses were built and decorated for others. Ruth clearly remembers the one earmarked for Lowell Thomas. "Lowell Thomas was in Pawling, New York," she explains, "and we were over on the Hudson River," some distance away. "His chauffeur was going to pick up the house," she goes on, "but something happened and he couldn't come. So we put four posts on the corners of the board, covered the whole thing with clear plastic, and sent it in the mail. Would you believe that the Post Office got it to him without a single thing broken," she marvels.

Later Bill McChesney, Jr., and his wife Deni continued the family tradition by inviting friends to help decorate a castle that Bill, who calls himself a "frustrated architect," had built out

of plywood. Each year the guest list increased, as did the complexity of the models to be decorated.

Several years ago, Bill and Deni McChesney decided to turn this family tradition into a fund-raiser for Historic Speedwell, a museum complex in New Jersey that includes eight historic structures. Each year, with the help of volunteers, Bill designs and constructs one hundred buildings. Special buildings are also designed by architects.

Volunteers mix up gallons of egg whites and hundreds of pounds of powdered sugar for the frosting. Several corporations sponsor models, some replicas of their own corporate headquarters. Donations are solicited from community groups, and families also sponsor and decorate candy houses.

The fund-raisers are hugely successful, raising $50,000 annually for Historic Speedwell and providing adults as well as children with an exciting pre-Christmas event. "I guess that was the beginning of my wanting to do miniature rooms," Ruth remarks.

# 2
# RUTH McCHESNEY

Ruth B. McChesney's story is the story of a miniatures collector with a mission. She intended from the beginning for her miniature rooms to be of museum quality. Many of them are already in museums in the United States and England. Her acquisitions began with one of the best, a French bureau plat or desk by Denis Hillman.

Ruth was born and grew up in the Chicago area. Her father, Edwin Balmer, was a successful and popular writer of fiction. One of his books, *The Indian Drum,* was a favorite of Teddy Roosevelt's. Another, *When Worlds Collide,* a science fiction story, was made into a movie and later provided ideas for the *Star Wars* trilogy.

*Nothing delights Ruth more than sharing her miniature rooms with others. She is shown here at the presentation of three of her rooms to Sewickley Academy, her sons' alma mater, where they are on permanent exhibit in the Campbell Gallery. The miniature rooms shown behind her are the French Transitional Room (left), the Covent Garden Supper Room (middle), and a Queen Anne-style dining room (right). Photo courtesy Ruth McChesney.*

Ruth attended the North Shore Country Day School. She recalls coming home for lunch to find the Arctic explorer Vilhjalmur Stefansson visiting, or Constance Bennett, a popular movie star of the period. "You never knew who you'd see. It was a very interesting childhood," she remembers.

When Edwin Balmer became editor of *Redbook* magazine, the family moved to Westchester, New York. Shortly thereafter, Ruth went off to Smith College in Northampton, Massachusetts.

At Smith, Ruth studied art history under Professor Van Vorenkamp, "a wonderful man," Ruth reminisces. "Through his classes I learned to love and identify period furniture." Also about this time, she developed what is known as a good eye and decided to become a professional photographer.

"I went to the Clarence White School of Photography in New York City after graduation from Smith," Ruth says. "Then I worked for about two years for a photographic studio that specialized in advertising work. It was interesting because I did all their set-ups for them." She had started freelancing and was photographing babies and young children by the time she met and married William S. McChesney.

"We met on the golf course," Ruth remembers. "I used to play tennis all the time, and I saw the best-looking men playing golf, so I thought I'd better get on the golf course," she laughs. "I was playing on the second hole with my father one day, and a nice foursome let us play through. I looked back at the foursome, he looked at me, and that was my husband."

Bill and Ruth McChesney had two sons. Bill, Jr., is married to Deni, a successful commercial artist, and lives in New Jersey, where he is a banker by vocation and has an avid interest in all things architectural. Tom is senior vice president of a real estate company in Pittsburgh and is married to Lisa, an accomplished designer of jewelry. Both sons display Ruth's miniature rooms in their homes and are very supportive of her work.

When the boys were about four and six years old, Bill McChesney was transferred by his company, Alcoa, from the New York area to Pittsburgh. He and Ruth bought a house in Sewickley Heights, not too far from where she lives now, and Ruth set about raising her children, doing volunteer work in the community, and doing needlework in her spare time.

She began to think about acquiring period furnishings when she learned that the McChesney home had been adapted from an early nineteenth-century house in Virginia called Bremo, a Jeffersonian house. "When we bought it," Ruth relates, "I decided I was going to try to put the furnishings in it that suited it."

About twenty-five years ago, several incidents led Ruth, either directly or indirectly, to become what she is today: a miniatures artisan and collector and a successful creator of museum-quality rooms. By far the most traumatic of those incidents was learning that her husband had an illness that would become increasingly more debilitating and could last for years. Bill McChesney lived with his illness for twenty years, dying in 1990.

Bill retired from Alcoa in 1970. For the next five years, while Bill was able, he and Ruth traveled often. "At this point, I was somewhat interested in miniatures," Ruth says. During one of their trips, Ruth began experiencing shoulder problems. A friend thought the pain might have been caused by carrying the heavy needlework canvases Ruth was working with and suggested switching to petit point. Ruth followed her friend's advice. In 1985 Ruth was awarded artisan status in the International Guild of Miniatures Artisans for her excellent petit point rugs.

Sometimes their travels took the McChesneys to miniatures shows. Ruth had purchased a veneered bureau plat created by Denis Hillman out of five different types of wood and had created a shadow box to showcase her first petit point rug. "Bill was very interested, too," she remembers, "so it worked out very well."

"My family had a few antiques around the house," Ruth remembers about her growing up years, "but there was never a room that was specifically one period. I think my interest in French furniture occurred because my mother and grandmother had a French desk with inlay that always intrigued me. I used to go and sit with my grandmother and study that desk, and I finally got one that reminds me of it.

"In 1980, on a trip to England, I was invited to Badger's Mount in Hailsham, Sussex, to meet Denis Hillman. He and his wife were most cordial, and I loved seeing his workshop. He took me, along with his dog," she remembers, "to a pub which as I recall was named Smuggler's Roost, relating back to a sort of prohibition years ago when there were tunnels

*This Louis XV bureau plat, built by Denis Hillman after the Gaudreaux piece at Versailles, was the first piece of miniature furniture Ruth acquired. It is one of only two made, has working locks with keys on the three drawers, and is built on an oak frame veneered with kingwood, purplewood, and a tulipwood inlay. The desk is shown on the right side of the Breteuil Salon (see 4, "Breteuil Salon"). Photo courtesy Ruth McChesney.*

from one pub to another. And, it's typically English to allow dogs in a bar.

"I'm more interested in the wood than I am in anything else," Ruth explains about her choices of furniture styles, "the carving of the wood and how it's made." Each of her rooms also contains a dog. "I am very fond of dogs. I think they make the room look lived in. Once I started doing it, people teased me about it, and I said I was going to have one in every room.

"Also, I think the biggest reason I did it was that by the time I was working on these rooms so much, I had given up my big house to go into an apartment and I couldn't have a dog. I also try to leave something a little bit askew in a room, or do something to indicate that someone has been using the room. It may be just a dented sofa

pillow or a book on a table, anything that indicates activity."

That bit of realism comes after the huge amount of research. Ruth takes great pains in designing rooms that will teach the viewer something about the period in which the full-sized room would have been created. She has never hesitated to seek the advice of people she considers experts in their field. "I was fortunate in learning from a marvelous man, Eugene Kupjack," Ruth says, "the problems of devising museum rooms, as well as how to light them and make them durable so they would continue to be in existence after twenty years."

It is interesting to note that Ruth buys miniatures of the highest quality not to keep for herself, but almost always with the intention of giving them away. She feels very strongly that miniatures should be shared, and she is doing everything in her power to make sure that hers are. Many of the rooms she has created are already in museums; others are under construction with just that destination in mind. It is, after all, her mission.

# Tudor Period

### 3
# TUDOR ROOM
*Circa 1586*

This Tudor room was inspired by a small dining room at Levens Hall, Westmoreland, an Elizabethan house built in the sixteenth century. The room was chosen primarily because of its interesting woodwork and intricate strapwork ceiling and was built for Ruth by the Kupjack Studio.

Ruth became interested in recreating a sixteenth-century room in miniature when she met Ivan Turner, the well-known English authority on the Elizabethan period who, with his wife Daphne, creates museum miniatures of the period. "He gave me great ideas about how to do Elizabethan rooms," Ruth relates, "and authenticated all the things I planned to put in the room. I appreciated that very much, as he is an

*The Tudor Room. Photo by Tom Barr.*

*The Tudor Room as an empty canvas, ready to be filled. Photo courtesy Kupjack Studios.*

*Ruth stitched the needlepoint cushion for this bench, which was built for her by John Ottewill. Photo by Nick Forder.*

excellent historian as well as a superb wood carver.

"He does remarkable reproductions," Ruth goes on, "which are only in museums. His wife is wonderful, too, and does magnificent needlepoint. It's unbelievable what she can do," says Ruth, a very fine needleworker herself. "She works on the tiniest scale I have ever seen."

Among the items Ivan Turner authenticated for this room are a pair of chairs, one of which was made by Barry Hipwell of Leicestershire, England. Ruth had already commissioned some of the furnishings from John Ottewill of Canada when she found what she calls "that wonderful chair."

Ruth first saw this Elizabethan chair on the cover of *Oak Furniture— The British Tradition* by Victor Chinnery.

The original chairs are a type called caqueteuse, after the French word for "gossiping," and were made for the mayor of Salisbury by Maurice Green, whose initials, MGM, and the date, 1622, are carved in the crest rail.

John Ottewill made the second MGM chair as well as the Jacobean court cupboard, which is five inches long and just over five inches high, and a bench for which Ruth created the needlepoint cover. He also built the Jacobean draw-leaf table and a Tudor chest. The Tudor coat of arms above the fireplace, adapted from an English original, was carved by Nicole Walton-Marble; the tigerware jug was made by Muriel Hopwood; and the mandolin was made by Ken Manning of Canada.

"Ken had made a lute for me," Ruth recalls, "a lady's lute which was absolutely the correct proportion, but

when we put it in the room, it looked too big, as is sometimes the case with miniatures. So, he made me a mandolin instead, which is a much smaller instrument and looked correct."

"I particularly love the dog warming himself by the fire," Ruth declares. He is a mastiff modeled by Karl Blindheim of Toronto, Canada. Ken Palmer, an English silversmith, made several pieces for the room. Porcelain items are by Elizabeth Chambers. Two of the decorative accessories Ruth used actually date back to her childhood.

"When I traveled to England and France with my family," she reminisces, "my governess would allow me to pick out little things to buy, and when I was five years old, I picked out a pair of crouching lions carved in ivory. They are now sitting on the mantel in this room and they not only look correct but have obvious ties to the British royal crest."

The chair cushions are one example of miniatures that are an illusion, not exactly what they appear to be. They were carved by Dick Smith. "I

*Court cupboard by John Ottewill, from right side of room. Photo by John Ottewill.*

came in one day," Dick recalls, "and Ruth said, 'we need some cushions.' I had some cotton suede cloth which we were going to use, but when you get down to that scale, that fabric has some thickness to it, and it just wasn't working. So Ruth gave me a couple of chunks of balsa wood and an X-acto knife and said, 'see what you can do.' It's really very flattering," Dick laughs, "that Ruth has such confidence in me."

He carved the cushions from that balsa wood, painted them, and "kind of dirtied them a little bit," Dick goes on, "and we put on the braid. You can see how the braid dips down on the front edge as if people had been sitting on it." Dick also added some aging to the room itself. "See the little bit of a dark spot on the second panel up on the door frame," he points out, "where hands might have touched it. We darkened the door around the latch, and added the smoke stains on the stone surround above the fireplace opening."

"We had great fun aging this room," Ruth concludes.

# BRETEUIL SALON

*Circa 1720*

It is called the Salon of the Four Seasons because of the tapestries it contains—four magnificent portieres of Gobelins tapestry of the Regency period, representing spring, summer, fall, and winter. It is a room that took ten years from concept to completion. And it is the room that contains Ruth's favorite piece of French furniture, the Hillman bureau plat.

When Ruth conceived the idea of doing an eighteenth-century French room in miniature, she went to France to look specifically for an extant room with original furnishings that she could copy. There are very few eighteenth-century rooms with original furnishings because, under French inheritance laws, family lands and buildings traditionally pass to the eldest son, while the furniture and other possessions are passed to siblings.

Ruth conferred with Serge Grandjean, then curator of decorative arts, the Louvre, and with Theodore Dell, the French furniture historian who cataloged the French collection for the Frick Museum in New York City. Both suggested rooms for her to see. After visiting several chateaux, Ruth decided that the Salon of the Four Seasons at the Chateau de Breteuil was the room she wanted to replicate.

The Chateau de Breteuil is located in the Chevreuse valley, southwest of Paris. Its current owner, the Marquis Henri-François de Breteuil, inherited and began restoration of the property in 1967. De Breteuil's noted ancestors include the state secretary of war for Louis XV. Although the chateau was falling into disrepair, it was one of very few chateaux that still contained original furnishings. One suite of furniture by Pierre Bernard, with needlepoint illustrating the fables of La Fontaine, was made for the chateau in 1771 and has never left it except for recent restoration.

Ruth designed the overall plan for the room, deciding which perspective would be most appropriate for viewing it, and arranged for the shell to be constructed. It is her photograph of the chateau's gardens, enlarged to the appropriate size, that can be seen through the doors on the right side of the room.

That photo was taken during Ruth's second visit to Breteuil, when she was accompanied by her sister. "The marquis and his wife invited us for lunch," she remembers, "and took such interest in the project that we arranged to meet later in New York once the room was under construction. We met at the home of Theodore Dell and showed the marquis and his master restorer the model and the furnishings that had been completed."

*The magnificent Salon of the Four Seasons from the Chateau de Breteuil. Photo by Tom Barr.*

*One of the tapestries stitched by Sharon Garmize especially for this room. Photo by Tom Barr.*

Ruth also began work on the miniature copy of a magnificent Savonnerie carpet, a needlepoint she is probably more proud of than any other she has done. She also stitched the covering for the two footstools in the room and researched and commissioned the pieces that would fill the room.

Sharon Garmize replicated the tapestries for which the room is named and stitched the petit point (or Saint Cyr point) upholstery for the gilded suite of furniture originally created by Pierre Bernard, which includes a sofa, a pair of bergères, and armchairs. The chandelier is also a copy of one that has been in the room since it was originally decorated around 1750, as is the petit point fire screen.

As work on the room progressed, Ruth learned that it would be accepted for permanent display at the Carnegie Museum of Art in Pittsburgh. At that point, the museum wanted to include a few other examples of eighteenth-century French furnishings, some from other rooms in the chateau, and two from museums in the United States and abroad. Ruth commissioned Kupjack Studios to prepare the room for museum display and to build several pieces of furniture for it.

In 1993 the Salon of the Four Seasons became part of the permanent display in the Ailsa Mellon Bruce Galleries at the Carnegie. Sarah Nichols, curator of decorative arts at the museum, was there when the room was installed. "I was delighted to be able to give a context to the collections that we have here," she says. "Because we don't have any period rooms in this museum, it's always a problem showing furniture because

*The scene outside the salon's glass doors is an enlarged view of the actual chateau's gardens. Dick Smith painted the four-panel screen after the original at the J. Paul Getty Museum in Malibu, California. Photo by Tom Barr.*

29

*Ruth stitched the magnificent Savonnerie carpet and the coverings for the footstools. Sharon Garmize copied the original upholstery for the suite of furniture in the room. Photo by Tom Barr.*

people don't really understand how it was used, where it was placed in a room, or the rooms that specific pieces went in.

"Obviously," Sarah goes on, "these rooms were quite different from rooms we have today, so our reason for accepting this room and placing it here was to give a context to the furniture in this gallery. There are a number of parallels that you can make between the objects in this room and the objects that we have here. People can look at this room to see how everything goes together, and then look at individual objects in the collection, such as the fire screen, the andirons, the console tables."

It has been many years since most museums installed full-sized period rooms, and for that reason, Sarah explains, "people can't see paneling and stucco work and carving and gilded work that made up the interiors of a room, so this is a wonderful image of that as well. People are just drawn to it. It really is very impressive. The workmanship is incredible."

Excellent workmanship has always been one of Ruth's primary criteria in the creation of a miniature room, and she chose some superb pieces, many of them one-of-a-kind, for this salon. Dick Smith painted the four-panel screen on the right side, copying an original screen displayed at the J. Paul Getty Museum in Malibu, California, which is covered with fabric woven at the Savonnerie factory in France.

Dick also painted several portraits for the room, including one of Gabrielle Emilie de Breteuil, an eighteenth-century woman who was very interested in science and the arts and was reportedly courted by Voltaire. Dick's portrait of Louis Auguste Le Tonnelier, Baron de Breteuil, hangs on the wall between the two doors and just above the only true antique in the room, which is a framed, hand-painted French card from the eighteenth century that Ruth bought in France years ago.

The chandelier, clock, and candlesticks were made by Wes Hart; Ron Stetkewicz created the fireplace accessories. Tom Poitras built a pair of console tables for the rear wall, and Dick Smith painted the faux marble tops.

A desk chair with 462 individual brass nail heads by Nicole Walton-Marble is copied from an original at the Getty Museum attributed to Etienne Meunier. The chair sits in front of a Louis XV bureau plat built by

Denis Hillman, copied from the original by Gaudreaux at Versailles. It is this desk, with its working locks and keys and exquisite workmanship, that is probably Ruth's favorite piece of furniture. It may have been the cornerstone of an idea that eventually became the Salon of the Four Seasons.

*Ruth's trademark dog in this room is a Pekinese, hand-carved in tiger's eye with black onyx eyes and nose and a rutile tongue, that she acquired in London. Photo by Tom Barr.*

# 5
# PORT ROYAL ENTRANCE HALL
## *Circa 1762*

*Ruth first met
Ian McCallum,
the late director
of the American
Museum in
Britain, at a
Palm Beach lun-
cheon in 1985.
While discussing
their mutual
interest in eigh-
teenth-century
furniture, he
mentioned the
museum's acqui-
sition of an
important
American high-
boy which, it
turned out, was
very similar to
the Philadelphia
Van Pelt highboy
Ruth had recently
purchased in
miniature from
Harry Cook.
That similarity
resulted in
Ruth's donation
of this room to
the museum.
Photo by
Mort Kaye.*

When Ruth funded a miniature room to be built by Eugene Kupjack and donated to Winterthur, she made a visit to that Delaware museum, the former home of Henry Francis duPont. "I became interested in doing another Winterthur room," she recalls, "and I particularly liked the Port Royal Entrance Hall." The hall is from a country house named Port Royal, built by Edward Stiles in 1762 and located north of Philadelphia.

Ruth commissioned the room and furnished it with a copy of an American Chippendale highboy, created in miniature by Harry Cook, the original of which is in Winterthur's Port Royal parlor. The Chippendale chairs with their unusual ribbon-back design were built by John Hodgson of England. Ruth stitched the rug. When the room was completed, she donated it to the American Museum in Britain, housed in Claverton Manor, an eighteenth-century country house outside Bath, England.

"Transporting that room to England was kind of fun," Ruth reminisces. "The easiest and least expensive way to do it was for me to buy a seat for it at half price. My sister and I put it on the seat between us for the trip over to London, and then the driver I always have there drove it up. It had first-class treatment all the way up to Bath," where the room now resides.

*This ribbon-back Chippendale armchair is one of a pair built by John Hodgson. Ruth stitched the needlepoint slip seats and personalized each one with an "M." Photo by Mort Kaye.*

# 6
# CECIL BEDROOM
### *Circa 1730*

*The Cecil Bedroom was Ruth's first museum donation. It was constructed by Kupjack Studios for Henry Francis duPont's Winterthur museum in Delaware. It is one of four miniature rooms built as exact copies of some of the most popular rooms in Winterthur and is often exhibited around the country at other museums and fine antique shows. Photo by Jay Kupjack.*

Louis XV-XVI Period

# 7

# FRENCH TRANSITIONAL ROOM

*Circa 1780*

*Ruth commissioned this room in honor of her daughter-in-law, Deni McChesney, who is of French descent. Photo by Mort Kaye.*

This may be the most traveled room in the collection. It has been displayed seven times at U.S. museums and antique shows and as far away as France, where it was shown at the Fourth Festival International de la Miniatura in Montilimar.

The late Eugene Kupjack built this room for Ruth. Although it is not a copy of a specific historical room, most of the furnishings are copied from their full-sized counterparts. The secretaire, for instance, with its Sèvres porcelain plaques and ormolu arabesques is after the Martin Carlin piece in the Wallace Collection in London. The original of Kupjack's japanned harpsichord (circa 1740), is at the Victoria and Albert Museum in London, and the small table with a Sèvres porcelain top is copied from an original Roger Vandercruse La Croix piece, also in the Wallace Collection in London. It is believed that La Croix did his finest work in the transitional style.

During the construction of this room, Ruth worked with Kupjack to choose and research the pieces it would contain. "The reason this is called a transitional room," she explains, "is that it contains both Louis XV and Louis XVI pieces. See, the legs are different. My daughter-in-law's family was French, and the clock and the perfumers on the mantel are copied from ones still in her family.

"I like the lighting," Ruth continues. "Kupjack was very good at lighting, using side lighting, which give a much better effect than lighting the front or back. He was a very knowledgeable man; he taught me a lot."

# 8
# SPENCER ANTEROOM
### *Circa 1792*

Spencer House in London was begun in 1756 by John, first earl Spencer, an ancestor of Diana, Princess of Wales. It remains the only great eighteenth-century townhouse intact in London today. The architect John Vardy designed the exterior and ground floor of the house, combining both Palladian and neoclassical elements. In this room, originally known as the little eating parlor or small dining room, he has rendered an unusual and spectacular apse. That particular architectural element was a major reason why this anteroom was chosen to be reproduced in miniature.

Knowing of her son Bill's strong interest in architecture, Ruth asked him several years ago "which single room in this world I would like to have her copy in miniature," Bill recalls now. He began his research in his own library of architectural books, focusing particularly on the Palladian and neoclassical styles because they were personal favorites, but it was during a trip to London in spring 1991 that Bill found the room you see here.

"In England, particularly in the eighteenth century," he explains, "individual builders of great houses and rooms were intimately interested in and excited by the new discoveries of Roman times that they had seen on

*Ruth and Bill McChesney at an exhibit of the anteroom at the Carnegie Museum of Art in Pittsburgh. Photo courtesy Ruth McChesney.*

*Ruth stitched this miniature copy of a sixteenth-century Persian carpet displayed in the Metropolitan Museum of Art in New York. Called the Tree and Garden Carpet, the original was woven during the reign of Shah Abbas. The miniature required approximately 106,000 stitches to complete. Photo by Tom Barr.*

their Grand Tours." These individuals, members of the English nobility, wanted to use these new styles in the elegant townhouses being built in London at that time. "For that reason, I was attracted to Lord Spencer and his wife, who set out to build the quintessential townhouse in the mid-eighteenth century."

When he visited Spencer House, Bill remembers, "I was struck by the scale of the anteroom, which is close to the double-cube spatial configuration first introduced by the architect Inigo

Jones in the Banqueting House nearby. It is not one of the grandest rooms in the building; in fact, it is quite intimate. However, when one steps back and thinks about the process of designing and building a massive townhouse over a twenty to thirty year period, this anteroom captures the dynamism and creative energy of the occupants." Vardy's little eating parlor became the anteroom in 1792 when the architect Henry Holland redesigned the interior of Spencer House, completing the up-stairs. It remains much the same today.

Once Bill had chosen the room he wanted his mother to reproduce, they had to decide on the most appropriate view into it. They settled on the vista from one end, which gives the viewer an opportunity to first gaze from right to left, starting with the magnificent apse. Then the viewer's eye takes in the Gainsborough portrait and the side table on the back wall and travels from there to the left where he sees through the windows the facade of Spencer House as seen from Green Park. "Then one has the opportunity to look again," Bill comments, "at the entrance way through the apse with a glimpse of the centaur sculpture in the Adam-style hallway, and finally moving back into the room, to appreciate the desk, the chandelier, and my mother's master-piece needlepoint rug."

After this room was chosen as her next project, Ruth began the meticulous and extensive research that is the basis of each of her rooms. She traveled to England, viewed the room, measured it, and conferred with Stephen Jones, the curator of Spencer House. He provided some of the photographs used during the building process and she took many others. "We even went to the London Museum to look at the Vardy drawings," Ruth comments. "He was one of the finest architects in England." Ruth also was able to get copies of the original floor plans and elevations for the room, which she passed along to her builder, Richard Shurtz. What they did not realize immediately, though, was that those original floor plans had been somewhat altered later in the room's existence.

"We weren't aware of that at first," Richard remembers. "The original room was made in a classical way, the dimensions based on pure Roman geometry. A semicircle was always an exact half-circle. The apse in that room went back in an exact half-circle, and the vault of the apse went up in the same way, which was a typical Roman motif. But," he goes on, "in the late eighteenth century, the hall was made larger. They actually took four feet away from the semicircular apse so it no longer was a semicircle, but was an oval instead, although the front stayed the same. That altered the geometry of all that coffering completely."

This architectural alteration was discovered when Richard built a mock-up of the room from the original plans. Building a mock-up is the first step in building the actual room, so as to have an accurate indication of the size the miniature room will be. When Ruth and Dick Smith examined the mock-up, they realized that the apse did not completely resemble the photographs they had, so Ruth contacted Stephen Jones again and asked for the measure-ment from the back of the apse to the front pilasters that form the base of the facade. It should have been ten feet, but was only six, "so we had to revise the entire thing," Richard continues.

"When you are trying to make cof-fering from two semicircles that are

*Wes Hart was commissioned to copy this elegant Georgian chandelier. He also built the gilded mirror over the desk. A gilt neoclassical table on the back wall and the pair of side chairs copied from originals by William Hallett (circa 1740) were constructed in miniature by Geoffrey Wonnacot. Photo by Tom Barr.*

identical," he explains, "it's very easy to do. Here's the secret to it: If you've got two perfect semicircles with something going up at 45 degrees and another thing crossing at 45 degrees, it will naturally diminish in size as it goes up. But, if you have two angles that are completely different, they don't want to do that naturally. They have to be forced to do that. Whoever re-did the coffering on the original room was a genius at geometry. All I did was copy what he did. Once we realized what was going on, I just forced my coffering to do the same thing his did."

It was the most complex part of the most difficult project Richard had ever worked on, although the ceiling was also somewhat complex because of the unusually deep cornice molding. "The original room is seventeen feet tall to the very top of the ceiling," he explains, "and that cornice, from the flat part of the ceiling to the bottom is almost two feet, six inches. That's how deep that molding is in real life," he marvels. Since he did have accurate measurements and clear, straight-on photographs of it, the construction of the molding went quite smoothly.

*Sunlight streams through the windows in this view of the left side of the anteroom. The draperies and desk chair are the work of Judee Williamson and Nicole Walton-Marble, and the desk was replicated in miniature by John Davenport. Photo by Nick Forder.*

Besides building the room itself with its unusual apse and lovely ceiling, Richard made all the picture frames and painstakingly applied all the gold leaf. "I had done gold leafing, but some of the gold leaf was literally just hair thin," he recalls about that part of the project. "The sizing you use, the glue for the gold leaf, has a tendency to spread itself like crazy, so to control that was very difficult to do." All told, Richard's part of this project took about a year to complete.

During that time, Ruth was researching the furnishings and other decorations to be used in the room. She

*John Davenport's mahogany knee-hole desk is similar to furniture made in 1740 by Vile and Cobb for the Royal Collection. Photo courtesy Ruth McChesney.*

commissioned Geoffrey Wonnacot, an English miniatures artisan, to build the gilt neoclassical side table on the back wall, the original of which is attributed to Sir William Chambers. Geoffrey also constructed the pair of side chairs, reproducing originals built by William Hallett in about 1740. John Davenport, another English miniatures artisan, created the handsome mahogany Chippendale desk on the left, reproducing it exactly. The original is similar to furniture made in 1740 by Vile and Cobb for the Royal Collection. The Paul de Lamerie ink stand (circa 1749–1750) on the desk was created by Peter Acquisto.

Wes Hart of Arizona reproduced the elegant Georgian glass chandelier and the gilded mirror between the two windows, which is in the style of Linnell, about 1766. Ruth suggested adding a sleeve to cover the chain supporting the chandelier. "I like to have the chain covered," she comments. "If

it were not covered, it would take away from the gilt on the ceiling, I think." Ruth stitched the carpet, which is a copy of a priceless Shah Abbas Persian rug from the sixteenth century that is displayed in the Metropolitan Museum of Art in New York. "It was too bright," she confides, "when we put it in the room, so I rubbed it with a little face powder in a suntan shade to make it look old. I could get it out if I had to; I didn't want to do anything permanent to it." Ruth estimates that there are some 106,000 stitches in that 8 x 15-inch carpet.

The window treatments were constructed by Judee Williamson and Nicole Walton-Marble of Arizona and finished by Dick Smith. "The curtain treatments are replicas of what is there today," Dick explains, "and the tassel fringe is individually hand-tied tassels, individually sewn on. The fabric is, I think, one of the most astounding things in Ruth's whole collection. I sent

Judee and Nicole a length of real silk damask and a yard of that cerulean blue taffeta. They photographed the damask, had it printed, and copied it to get a running repeat. Then they printed it in a slightly darker color on the blue taffeta to give the feeling of damask. Every detail in the real one is in the miniature through that photographic process.

"When the curtains arrived," Dick goes on, "the tassels all sort of flared out," because of the way they are made, and "because it is a fiber and has a body of its own. So, we got clear, water-based varnish and with a brush and a pair of tweezers, we soaked each tassel and then formed it so it hangs straight, the way a silk tassel would. Then we changed the shape of the curtain panels to appear as they are in the real anteroom, which are straight, hanging panels. To achieve the soft folds on the pleated curtains, we spray-glued aluminum foil between the face fabric and the lining, and then formed the folds around the thick leather cover of an antique dictionary. The aluminum foil, of course, holds the shape," he relates.

Dick also painted the five portraits in the room, all of them reproductions of Spencer family portraits. Two of the paintings are of Lady Charles Spencer, originals by Reynolds; and one is of Georgianna, Duchess of Devonshire, a daughter of John Spencer, the original by Thomas Gainsborough. A portrait of Colonel George Grey is copied from an original painted by Anton Raphael Mengs, about 1745. "He was the man who found the architect Vardy for John Spencer," Dick points out. Gainsborough painted the original half-length portrait of John, first earl Spencer. Dick also created the busts of Homer and Hesiod that sit on marbleized pedestals, which were copied from originals in the Capitoline Museum in Rome. "The two busts were taken from two that are on the mantelpiece in what is known as the Palm Room in Spencer House," he comments, "so they do have precedent in the house."

The flower arrangement was created by Jean Wickwire, and the candelabra are by Kupjack. Williamson Walton-Marble made the desk chair using the same fabric as was used for the curtains. "[Judee Williamson has] even got the tufts on the back of the chair," Dick observes. "People think of tufted upholstery as Victorian, which it is not. In the eighteenth century that was the only way of keeping the stuffing in the back of a chair from slipping to the bottom."

The decanter contains "a good English claret-colored liquid," Dick explains, installed with the help of a tiny syringe. "When we tried to pour the liquid in," he recalls, "even though the throat is hollow, we couldn't get the air displaced, so Ruth asked her doctor for the smallest syringe he had and we used that." The basaltware urn in the niche was copied from the stone urns on the parapet of Spencer House. "A dog in every room is Ruth's signature," Dick points out. "Standing at the door is a dark-brindle greyhound," created by Karl Blindheim of Toronto, Canada.

# 9

# JEFFERSON HALL AND DINING ROOM

## *Circa 1810*

While I was at the American Museum in Britain, delivering the Port Royal Entrance Hall," Ruth remembers, Ian McCallum, then the museum's director, expressed an interest in acquiring a Jeffersonian miniature room for the museum. "It so happened," she goes on, "that my house in Sewickley was built by a man who adapted Bremo, a house on the James River near Charlottesville, Virginia. Bremo was supposed to have been designed by Thomas Jefferson, but was later found to have been designed by a contemporary, John Neilson, in the federal style."

The house, built about 1810, has such Jeffersonian features as parquet floors, keystone arches, and triple-hung windows. Ruth had already commissioned a room box based on her own hall and dining room, so she set about researching the period and the proper furnishings, "to make it more in the federal style," she explains, "so it would be proper to send over to England. The Kupjacks helped me re-do that room and get it into condition.

*The Jefferson hall and dining room as it appears on exhibit at the American Museum in Britain. Photo courtesy of the American Museum.*

It was my second donation to the American Museum in Britain, and it has been a very popular room."

There are several antique miniatures in the room, including a porcelain table and pieces of carved jade. The Tang horse on the mantel is by Le Chateau Interiors; Peter Acquisto created the dining room chandelier. Ron Stetkewicz made the fireplace fender and tools, and Denis Hillman of England built the drop leaf table in the hall. The handsome tall case clock in the hall, copied from the original built by Simon Willard, around 1800, was made of Santo Domingo mahogany by Ernie Levy. Ruth stitched the needlepoint rugs, one of which is a copy of a rug she owned at the time, and the chair seat covers.

In this room, Ruth's trademark dog is a netsuke. "That comes from China," she points out, "and it is very hard to find a netsuke that looks real, but this is a real netsuke dog, and he's adorable."

*Bremo, a federal-style house in Virginia, inspired the architect who built the McChesney home in Sewickley, Pennsylvania, where Ruth lived when she commissioned the room box that became the Jefferson hall and dining room. A unique feature of the house is the fact that the entrance shown is on the second floor. The first floor, where the hall and dining room are located, is below because the house was built on a slope. Photo courtesy Ruth McChesney.*

# 10
# COVENT GARDEN SUPPER ROOM
## *Circa 1810*

Ruth calls this room "a flight of fancy," an interpretation of what a late seventeenth-century or early eighteenth-century private box and supper room at Covent Garden might have looked like. Richard Shurtz, who built the room, recalls, "I was browsing in the library one day and came across a book of eighteenth-century floor plans, which included plans for Covent Garden. There were no renderings of elevations at all, but I knew Covent Garden had supper rooms, and I thought it was an interesting idea, so I just invented the entire room."

To further the illusion of depth in this room, the chairs in the box are three-quarter-inch scale (one inch equals one foot is the scale of the rest of the furniture) and the proscenium, that part of the stage in front of the curtain, is slightly narrower than it would have been. "A smaller stage," Ruth points out, "gives the feeling that it is sixty feet away from you, which it would be."

Ruth's trademark dog in this setting happens to be green jade because "this is not a real dog," she says. "A dog wouldn't have been at the theater."

*A supper room at Covent Garden. Photo by Mort Kaye.*

# FEDERAL PARLOR

*Early Nineteenth Century*

*This small federal parlor features a portrait of Ruth's granddaughter Marni above the fireplace. While not a reproduction of any specific room, this parlor is typical of a room in an American federal period house furnished with various styles of furniture. The Queen Anne chess table and Chippendale side chairs were built by John Hodgson, and the two small paintings hanging above that grouping were purchased by Ruth at the Singing Tree in London. Ruth stitched the rug and the seat cover for the Hepplewhite armchair made by Betty Valentine. The pug dog sitting on a small rug below the window is a Viennese bronze. Photo by Tom Barr.*

*A close-up of
the portrait of
Marni, which
was painted
by Dick Smith.
Photo by
Tom Barr.*

# 12
# CHESAPEAKE ROOM
## *Circa 1815*

A sea captain in the early nineteenth century might have looked forward to coming home to a room like this. Ruth designed this room for her son Tom who had served in the Navy. "I had great pleasure assembling all the things for it," she reminisces. "We put many things into it that had a nautical connection."

Two of those items, of course, are ship models. Patricia Crawford created Nelson's flagship, the HMS *Victory*, using her own dog's hair for the rigging because silk thread was not strong enough. The model is an inch and a quarter long. Ron Stetkewicz's model of the USS *Constitution* in full sail can be seen in the alcove.

"I try to remember to send photographs of my rooms to the various artisans who worked on them," Ruth comments. "It was especially gratifying to be able to show pictures of this room to Ron Stetkewicz, who made many, many things for this room. This particular room seems to be a hit with men." Among the nautical and other items Ron created for the room are the fire fender and tools, a small telescope on the desk, a telescope on a tripod, the barometer on the right rear wall, a magnifying glass, and carved ducks below the painted panels on the left.

Richard Shurtz built the room in the early 1980s and then did a renovation of it ten years later. "It was an early room by my standards," he comments, "and my work had progressed enough so that it looked just a little bit crude to me. I remade the oval arch so it is a little more accurate and authentic, re-did the painted wall murals a little bit, and made the moldings more refined." He also enlarged the window. "The original window was much too small and the glazing bars were a little too clumsy."

The original oval arch was much heavier in its architectural detail. "This is much more in keeping with this period, the early nineteenth century," Dick Smith explains. "There is an arch similar to it at Monticello." Dick also recommended a different paint technique. "I suggested doing the flat sections of the wall in an off-white, a broken white," he remembers, "that would enhance the moldings and add to the architectural flavor of the room, which I think it does very nicely."

Harry Smith of Camden, Maine, whose exceptional work is in fine galleries, museums, and private collections all over the world, created the stunning bird's-eye maple highboy. The American Queen Anne side chair by Gerald Crawford is copied from the original at Winterthur. In the right foreground is a brass standing birdcage by Alex Freed of London, England. Ruth stitched the rug and the

*The Chesapeake Room, typical of a room in an American federal period house. Photo by Tom Barr.*

needlepoint covering for the Sheraton settee in the alcove. She also found a grouping of Viennese bronze dogs to resemble her son's dachshunds, and Dick Smith painted them for her.

"Since this was made for Tom and Lisa, Ruth's son and daughter-in-law," Dick relates, "I painted them like their real dogs. One is red, one black with red points, and the third, while purebred, is black with red points and many silver gray spots. This dog is called a dapple. No," he laughs, "the paint is not wearing off. That's the way he looks."

The three flowerpots on the window ledge in the alcove are also Austrian bronzes, sitting on saucers

Dick Smith remembers well. "I was on the way over here one morning when we were setting the room up for the final time, and someone mentioned to me that I was missing a button on my coat sleeve. Then Ruth brought out the three flowerpots to put on the window sill, but she said, 'wait a minute, no one would put flowerpots on a window sill without saucers.'

"Something clicked in my mind," Dick continues, "and I asked her if she had a button box. We found three buttons, and I painted them terra cotta." Had he not been aware of his missing button, though, Dick might not have thought of this clever improvisation.

*A trio of Viennese bronze dachshunds was painted by Dick Smith to resemble the real dogs owned by Tom McChesney. Photo by Nick Forder.*

*Tom McChesney with two of the models for the room's miniature dogs. Photo courtesy Ruth McChesney.*

*Nelson's flag-ship, HMS Victory, was reproduced in a miniature only an inch-and-a-quarter long by Patricia Crawford. She used dog's hair for the rigging when thread proved to be unsuitable. The ship model is displayed to the left of the arch in the Chesapeake Room. Photo courtesy Ruth McChesney.*

# 13
# WILPEN HALL PARLOR
## Circa 1895

A 1907 photograph was used to create in miniature the parlor of a well-known large stone country house called Wilpen Hall. William Penn Snyder, a Pittsburgh industrialist, built Wilpen Hall in Sewickley, Pennsylvania, in 1895. Today his grandson and his wife live there.

Ruth wanted to do one room in the Edwardian turn-of-the-century style. "This room typifies the period and was the one that appealed to me," Ruth recalls. "I know the Snyders and knew I would enjoy doing it."

The miniature room is an accurate representation of the way the room looked at the time the photograph was taken in 1907. "We copied as many of the furnishings as we possibly could," Ruth adds. "We even got all the family pictures to put in the little frames."

The room itself was built by William and Frances Bowen of South Carolina and is filled with the work of many artisans. It also contains several antique accessories, such as the pair of Baxter prints, one of the Crystal Palace and the other of Balmoral Castle, that

*The Wilpen Hall Parlor, an Edwardian-style room. Photo by Bob Basl.*

hang on one wall. There are also Baxter prints of Queen Victoria and Prince Albert in the room.

Ernie Levy created both the tall case clock and a mantel clock. Other furniture was built by Ferd Sobol, George Passwaters, John Davenport, Ibes Gonzales, Denis Hillman, Terry Rogal, and Nic Nichols. Sharon Garmize stitched needlepoint cushions

and a bolster, and Ruth made the rugs. Silver items were created by Cini, Obadiah Fisher, and Stuart McCabe.

Other decorative accessories were made by an international group of artisans that includes Francis Whittemore, Wes Hart, Robert Olszewski, Deborah McKnight, the late Ron Benson, and Mary Dudley Cowles, among others.

# 14
# SNYDER SITTING ROOM
## *Circa 1900*

Called the small Snyder room because of the portrait it contains, this room was originally constructed by Hal Weston and remodeled by Richard Shurtz. "We added the ceiling and ceiling cove," Richard explains. "It had no ceiling at all. We put in the fireplace and added the window wall, so basically we made it into a different room."

The portrait hanging above the fireplace is of Mrs. William P. Snyder, Jr., approximately 1950, and was painted by Marjorie Adams after the original portrait by Madame Elizabeth Shoumatoff, an artist who was completing a portrait of Franklin D. Roosevelt at the time of his death in 1945. "She did quite a bit of work here in Sewickley," Dick Smith explains. "I think this was one of her best."

The original portrait hangs in the sitting room at Wilpen Hall in Sewickley Heights, Pennsylvania, near Mrs. Snyder's William and Mary–style desk, which John Davenport, an English artisan, has faithfully copied in miniature for this setting, using walnut inlaid with boxwood stringing.

Dick Smith devised the window treatment, and Ruth made the cording trim. "This happened to be a real-sized fabric that had a scale we thought would do well in a miniature room," he explains, "so I covered the wall and made the valance and curtains."

The small Snyder Sitting Room features a portrait of Mrs. William P. Snyder, Jr., and her Dutch desk. The full-sized originals of both are in the family home, Wilpen Hall, in Sewickley, Pennsylvania. Photo by Nick Forder.

## 15
# TOM'S LIBRARY
### *Circa 1920*

*This miniature room, Tom's Library, was adapted by Kupjack Studios from an actual room in the home of Tom and Lisa McChesney and was furnished by Ruth McChesney. Photo by Tom Barr.*

When Tom and Lisa McChesney bought their current Pittsburgh house, they knew it needed considerable redecorating, but one room in the house made it all worthwhile. It is a small oak-paneled library with leaded glass windows inset with stained glass crests. The original room was added onto the house in the 1920s.

"I walked into this room," Tom remembers, "and saw my school seals on the windows. I went to Andover and Princeton, and if I had gone to business school, it would have been Harvard. My grandfather and uncle went to Harvard." The stained glass crests in the windows represent those schools. "I just said, 'wow, I love this room.' So, about four years ago when my mother wanted to make a room for us, I suggested this room, and here it is." Ruth comments, "I love this room because it has all my children's things in it. Even the ceiling is exactly the same."

*This Chippendale marble-top table built by Tom Poitras sits in a niche at left in the miniature room. It is done in the style of William Kent and is constructed of mahogany. Photo by Tom Barr.*

*John Davenport's miniature davenport desk is built of walnut and features a gold-tooled leather writing surface, a brass gallery, and ivory escutcheons. Photo by Tom Barr.*

*A Queen Anne settee built by Nicole Walton-Marble has upholstery hand-painted by Dick Smith after a 1730 English tapestry. Photo by Tom Barr.*

Kupjack Studios built the miniature room, replicating the three crests on the window on the left and adding the crests of the schools Tom and Lisa's two children attended to the window on the right. Among the pieces of furniture Ruth purchased for the room are a davenport desk by John Davenport and a table by Denis Hillman. Terry Rogal made the magazine rack and a pair of Queen Anne chairs, and Nicole Walton-Marble built the sofa, on which Dick Smith painted an upholstery design copied from an eighteenth-century English tapestry.

Tom Poitras made the Chippendale marble-top table for the room, and Mary McGrath's birds can be seen on the built-in shelves on either side of the fireplace. Ruth stitched the rug, and her trademark dog in this room is a Viennese bronze. Ruth and Lisa were excited about the framed selection of miniature shells acquired from Ron Stetkewicz to hang on one wall. "I love that," Ruth comments. "It's quite fun."

*This Sheraton
sewing table by
Denis Hillman,
shown both open
and closed, has a
working lock
with key and a
fitted interior.
Photos courtesy
Ruth McChesney.*

# Louis XVI Revival Period

## 16
# NISSIM DE CAMONDO HALL
### *Circa 1920*

This spectacular stair hall is Ruth McChesney's current project, her work in progress. Richard Shurtz has built the room and continues to work on the architectural details necessary to complete it. The room is copied from the stair hall in the Musée Nissim de Camondo in Paris, which was built as a private house by Comte Moise de Camondo between 1911 and 1914. The architect René Sergent modeled the building on the Petit Trianon at Versailles, which was built by Jacques Ange Gabriel for the Marquise de Pompadour, the mistress of Louis XV.

The room Ruth chose to have replicated in miniature was described in *Antiques* magazine in October 1995 as

*The Nissim de Camondo stair hall, in progress. Photo by Tom McChesney.*

*A view of the upper section of the Nissim de Camondo stair hall. Photo by Tom McChesney.*

*This two-drawer Louis XV commode, after the original in the Musée de Beaux Arts in Paris, was built by Kupjack Studios and painted by Dick Smith. It is placed in the niche on the left side of the stairs beneath an arch-topped painting, also by Dick Smith, copied from an original oil on canvas landscape by Hubert Robert. Photo by Tom Barr.*

A late eighteenth-century chased and gilt bronze candelabra after the original by Jean-François Leleu in 1761 was made by Wes Hart. Each of the chain links in the center section is thinner than a strand of hair. The miniature candelabra sits on the commode in the niche at left. Photo by Tom Barr.

A long-case clock, (circa 1780), with works by LePaute, Royal Clockmaker, inspired this miniature by Wes Hart, which stands on the landing. The clock is oak and mahogany with chased and gilt bronze and is exquisitely detailed. Photo by Tom Barr.

In the center of the stair hall is a lantern copied exactly from one on the second floor of the original stair hall. The miniature was made by Wes Hart and includes the shield at the top to deflect smoke from the candles. Photo by Tom Barr.

"all pale and silvery gray, gilt-bronze sconces enrich the walls and the glimpses of a fine, late seventeenth-century Gobelins hanging high on the wall anticipates the splendor of the State rooms, but the real focus of attention is Sergent's essentially austere architectural design."

The magazine also comments that "the cool, high entrance hall is dominated by a fine statue of a nymph and cherub attributed to Simon Louis Boizot, 1743–1809." While that statue was being modeled in miniature by Le Chateau Interiors in Louisiana, Ruth placed a photograph of it in the room to help give the room perspective (see 20, "How-to Tips and Techniques").

Other works have been commissioned specifically for this room as well, and some of the items have been completed. A wine cooler filled with Jean Wickwire's flowers occupies a shallow niche. A velvet dog house from Le Chateau Interiors, modeled after one supposedly owned by Marie Antoinette, sits nearby. Wes Hart made the sconces, the barometer, and the lantern, which was copied from one most recently owned by Henry Francis duPont.

"From a lighting point of view," Dick Smith comments, "this is probably going to be one of the most interesting rooms Ruth has done." The room appears to be intended for more sophisticated lighting than most miniature rooms by virtue of its design, and planning the proper lighting has been an ongoing effort.

"When we started this room," Richard Shurtz recalls, "we knew that this was going to be something we were going to do a little differently. We're going to have real stage lighting, subtle light in the foreground and then the background is going to be the brightest part." Background lighting spills down the stairs from large windows at the top, and side lighting on the lower level creates an interesting light and shadow effect on the flower arrangement.

Richard created the stair railing of gilded and painted iron; the niche is carved plaster over wood. "It goes back in an oval shape," he explains, "and after I got the oval just the way I wanted it, I started doing plaster on top of it." The result is just one detail, of course, but because of the lighting, an important one.

"It's not unlike stage design," Richard believes, "in that you rely on lighting to make the things you do actually more delicate than they really are. This is not to say that construction is not the most important thing, but you can do so much with lights, to direct people's attention here instead of there, for instance. You can, in fact, change the whole personality of a room with lighting."

*The original
Nissim de
Camondo stair
hall. Photo
courtesy Ruth
McChesney.*

# 17
# FRENCH ANTIQUE SHOP
## *Circa 1920*

*A view of the left side of the antique shop, an imaginary establishment filled with miniature treasures. Photo by Nick Forder.*

This French antique shop might be found in Paris today, but it is not an actual replica of an existing establishment. "I have an old reference book on French interiors," Dick Smith explains, "and we combined elements from a couple of rooms. The whole facade of the door wall came from one room. Then the room itself with the pilasters and so forth came from another room. But it's all Louis XVI period."

Richard Shurtz built the room, including the intricate concealed door on the right-hand side. "It was my idea to use the concealed door," Dick says, "because it is so typical in classical architecture. Real ones, the best ones, are on a spindle, and the vertical edges are on a canted angle, so that when the door is closed, all you see is the line

going up the baseboard, following around the paneling, and it just works out beautifully."

The effect is achieved, Dick continues, because in the full-sized door "the spindle would be maybe four inches in from where the hinge would normally be, so it would spin from there and you would not need to make a double 45-degree cut on the chair rail and the skirting."

Dick describes the lighting for this room as "ingenious." The moldings on the ceiling are arranged like a grid and attached to a piece of milk-white Lucite installed below the light source. "It's almost, I think, the best lit room because you don't see the light source, you're not really aware of it, and it just lights the whole thing." The design for the ceiling was illustrated in

Dick's reference book, although "it's not normally thought to be in a Louis XVI-period room." "But, being no particular room or from any particular building, we did take a few liberties with it."

This French antique shop is filled with treasures both old and new. There are six pieces of furniture created by the renowned Denis Hillman, an English artisan, including his jewel coffer on stand made of tulipwood, holly, and ebony veneered on oak. Its tiny lock and key actually work. It is lined in silk damask, and the outside is decorated with copies of Sèvres porcelain plaques bordered in turquoise blue. The original full-sized piece is in the Metropolitan Museum of Art in New York.

Denis Hillman also created the Louis XVI desk in tulipwood with

*The right-hand side of the antique shop shows the concealed door typical in classical architecture. Photo by Nick Forder.*

*This jewel coffer on stand, shown both open and closed, was built in miniature by Denis Hillman. He used tulipwood, sycamore, holly, and ebony veneered on oak to construct the piece. It is ornamented with porcelain Sèvres-type plaques, and the stand is fitted with a writing desk and drawer. The original was made by Martin Carlin and is in the Metropolitan Museum of Art. Photos courtesy Ruth McChesney.*

marquetry, called a "Bonheur-du-Jour," and the Louis XV commode on the right inlaid with macassar ebony and stringing in boxwood and cross-banded in macassar ebony on a mahogany veneer.

Hillman's upholstered pieces in this setting are the Louis XV canapé or sofa, upholstered in tapestry, and two fauteuils or armchairs. One is Louis XV-style, upholstered in tapestry, and the other is Louis XVI, upholstered in flowered brocade.

Kupjack Studios created the Louis XV commode on the left, copied from an original in the Musée des Beaux Arts in France. Dick Smith finished the veneered chinoiserie lacquered panels. John Davenport, another well-known English artisan, made the lady's desk located toward the back of the room on the left; and Peter Acquisto, a fine

miniatures silversmith from New Mexico, created the monteith bowl with tray and cups that sits in the back center of the room.

Other accessories, including gold serving pieces, were made by Kupjack Studios. The two paintings on either side of the room are eighteenth-century antiques, as are the pair of paintings on ivory that hang on the left toward the back.

"My love of miniatures," Ruth comments, "stems from my love of all art made of carved wood. Therefore, the small inlays by Denis Hillman and the unusual wood combinations used by John Davenport beckon to my taste. I tend to buy them whether I need them for a particular setting or not. Proof of this is the fact that I have six Denis Hillman pieces and two by Davenport in this antique shop."

# 18
# MARNI'S ROOM

Marni's Christmas Room was Ruth's gift to her grand-daughter when Marni was eight years old. A candy house rests on top of the highboy by John Hodgson. Ruth stitched the needlepoint rug, pillow, and covering for the roundabout chair by Betty Valentine. C. J. Traill-Hill built the pair of chairs with oval backs. Photo by Tom Barr.

# 19
# MIRROR VIGNETTE

*A view of the back of the Ernie Levy toilet mirror. Photo courtesy Ruth McChesney.*

# 20
# HOW-TO TIPS AND TECHNIQUES

*The inner walls of the Nissim de Camondo stair hall early in the construction phase. Ruth uses mock-ups and photographs to indicate where various elements will be located. Photo by Tom McChesney.*

Constructing a miniature room of lasting quality is not an easy task. Among the factors to be considered are the durability of materials used for the room itself and everything in it and the effect of heat and light over time. With several rooms already in museums, and others going there eventually, Ruth McChesney has learned exactly how to create a museum-quality miniature setting. Dick Smith also has

expertise to share. And Richard Shurtz can explain how the rooms themselves are built. The following information is based on principles that were known and products that were available in 1996.

## Building the Box

"You have to know the size of everything, the way an architect would,

before you start," Richard cautions. "The first thing to do is a floor plan, so I will know exactly what the interior measurement of the finished room is going to be because I have to build what I call a skeleton. It's just like a rib cage, a system of hardwood ribs going up the sides and across the top.

"Then you attach the walls to the rib cage," Richard goes on, "and if you know the final interior measurements, you compensate for the thickness of the walls and how thick the moldings will be. The ribs also hide the wiring; some of them are actually routed out so you can get wiring to any side."

Ruth's rooms are actually a box within a larger box. One of the factors that determines the size of the outer box is the lighting. Once the ribs are in place, says Richard, "I start arranging, front to back. I begin cutting walls and building the room the same way an architect would do it. You have window openings and then you do the framing the same way a carpenter would. You end up with a box that looks like a minimalist interpretation of a room, and then you start adding the embellishments, as it were": moldings, paneling, trim, whatever woodwork is appropriate for the period of the room.

## Lighting and Other Electrical Concerns

"If you are going to do a miniature room and you want to keep it for any length of time," Ruth cautions, "you must light it properly."

Lighting creates heat. "You have to be careful about air circulation," Richard comments. The Breteuil room, for instance, has an air conditioner that comes on whenever the lights are on and "can maintain a steady 72 degrees in that room at all times, no matter how long the lights are on.

"In the Spencer House room," Richard continues, "the light created a glare on the photograph seen from the windows. When you looked at it you immediately knew it was a photograph on paper, so what we did was attach shades to the Plexiglas tubes the lights are in, on the sides facing the photograph, just like stage lights, to cut the glare down a little bit."

Plexiglas tubes are used around every light in every room Ruth creates. They funnel the heat up to the top of the box, away from the furnishings and parts of the room that could be damaged by heat. In some cases, Ruth has an air conditioner installed in the shell surrounding the room. All the rooms that are now on permanent display in museums are air conditioned. "A very small solid-state unit is made for that, called Koolatron," she comments. The Koolatron unit is readily available.

Once the rooms are finished, lighted, and air conditioned, they are completely sealed. This eliminates dust, but it also creates a housekeeping problem: how do you clean the silver? "The only person I know of who makes silver that will not tarnish is Peter Acquisto," Ruth remarks, "so I always buy from him if the room is going into a museum. He uses a chemical to take the copper from the surface of the silver so it will not tarnish."

"Denglass is used on the face of the room to eliminate ultraviolet rays," Richard explains. "This does not alter colors, and is also nonglare."

## Materials

Richard builds the exterior box and the walls of each room out of

*This caned French fauteuil de bureau built by Nicole Walton-Marble illustrates Ruth's request for pegs on the furniture she commissions for her period rooms. The pegs will fit into holes drilled for them in the floor when a room is being completed for permanent display, then glued down to prevent the furniture from moving around. Photo by Tom Barr.*

medium-density overlay plywood made with "non-water-soluble glue," he explains. "It's very easy to get, it has a very smooth surface, and it is made for outdoor signs. You get no checking of the plywood over a very, very long period of time."

"According to the research center on the materials of the artist and conservator at Carnegie Mellon University in Pittsburgh," Dick has learned, "either oil or acrylic paint may be used. This, however, with the proviso that acrylic paint has been around for about forty years, and beyond that nothing is known about its durability."

Eugene Kupjack did not use glues with a petroleum base, according to his son Hank. He used Elmer's casein glue, which is the glue that Ruth recommends. If paper is to be used, it should be acid-free, such as a cotton rag paper that will not change color or deteriorate over a long period of time.

When Ruth commissions furniture for a room, she requests that each artisan add pegs to the bottom of each item. "The reason for that," Dick explains, "is that there is a certain amount of vibration in almost any building and over a year's time, furniture in a miniature room will start walking." And Ruth adds, "moving

any of these rooms can jar them, so you want them permanent." Once a room is completed, "because of the pegging and gluing everything down," Dick remarks, "you can turn it upside down and, with the exception of the chandelier, not a thing will move."

## Fooling the Eye

Diminishing perspective means, basically, that items that are farther away are smaller than items that are closer. In a miniature setting that might be twelve inches deep, you have to somehow fool the eye into thinking the room is deeper. Ruth usually does this in one of two ways: by arranging the furniture to compensate or by putting delicate items in the back. "I feel that the piece of furniture in the back," Ruth says, "if it is made in the exact miniature size, would be too dominant, so I try to put any large piece to the side or in the front. If I have a table in the back, for instance, I try to make it a rather delicate style, as you can see in the Spencer room."

The Covent Garden room illustrates how to create depth by using smaller scale items in the back of the setting. The chairs on the balcony are actually three-quarter-inch scale because one-inch scale, which is the scale for the rest of the furnishings, would look too close. "It's all our perception," Ruth says.

Color also plays a part in creating depth in a room, Dick Smith believes. "As you go toward the back, the color should become a little paler, to add depth. The color should be more intense toward the front of the room and get paler toward the back. In the Chesapeake room, for instance, we painted the flat part of the wall a slightly darker white to enhance the moldings, but the little corridor behind it was painted even paler than the room itself to give an exaggerated sense of depth."

Furniture, too, can fool the eye, depending on the circumstances. "I don't care what room it is," Ruth comments, "you don't find all the materials in the room perfectly clean and neat. If people have been living there, they look a little bit worn. I think many people make rooms that look as if they bought a whole set of furniture in a store, all equally new, all equally bright.

"So, just as I put a little bit of powder into a rug [in the Spencer House room] to make it older, when I'm working with materials, I put a little dirt on my hands and allow it to get onto the material so it looks as though it has been used."

In the Breteuil room, Dick made the elbow pads on the sofa and chairs of plastic wood, painting them to match the upholstery. "He put a little dent in each one," Ruth confides, "and they don't look peculiar that way, they look as though they had been used."

"Years ago," Dick quips, "a friend of my mother's who was a commercial artist told me to always remember: If it's right and it looks right, it's right. But, if it's right and it looks wrong, it is wrong. And, if it's wrong and it looks right, it's also right." Sage advice.

# 21
# DICK SMITH

Richard C. Smith is an interior designer by profession and a miniaturist by virtue of his association with Ruth McChesney. "In the last nine years, when my rooms were first being placed in museums, Dick Smith has been my invaluable right-hand support," Ruth remarks. "I could not have completed these rooms by myself with the assurance that all aspects had been considered."

The collaboration began with a curtain predicament, Dick remembers. "The woman who makes my curtains called me one day and said she had a client who was having trouble with some curtains. She said, 'you know Mrs. McChesney makes dollhouses'; she didn't understand about these things. And she didn't have time to go over, would I go, so I said, sure, and came over and we got the problem solved."

Later, there was discussion about whether to use curtains in the Breteuil room. "Then I marbleized some tabletops for that," Dick continues, "and one day Ruth learned that the person who was going to do the paintings was not going to be available, and I said, well, I paint portraits but I haven't done anything in miniature size. If you want, I'll do one for you." He painted the portrait, Ruth liked it, and Dick Smith has since painted a dozen or so miniature portraits for Ruth's miniature rooms.

Dick's knowledge of antiques and the decorative arts and his familiarity with color, line, and design, as well as his status as a "neophyte in the field," as he calls himself, have added an extra dimension to each of the projects he has worked on with Ruth. "You just don't know what you can do until you do it," he says. And Ruth adds: "With his artistic abilities and knowledge of period furnishings, we have made a great pair. He came along at just the right time."

*Along with the dozen or so miniature portraits and paintings Dick Smith has completed for Ruth's period rooms is this special one, a recent Christmas gift to her. Dick borrowed photographs of Ruth in her 40s, and, unbeknownst to her, painted her as Marie Antoinette. Photo by Tom Barr.*

# 22
# RICHARD SHURTZ

One might say that Richard Shurtz has found the niche in life he was always meant to have. "I wanted to be a stage set designer," he admits. But Richard followed the more "sensible" course in art school, leading to a teaching career. He majored in fine arts at Carnegie Mellon University in Pittsburgh, earning an master of fine arts in painting and design. And he spent the first ten years of his career teaching art. Then, looking for new challenges, and feeling like a "frustrated stage designer," he says, Richard discovered miniatures. Some time after that, Ruth McChesney discovered him.

Richard began building miniature room boxes and successfully selling them at shows during the early 1980s. These boxes were enhanced with all-handcrafted architectural details that made them much more interesting to collectors than the plainer ones previously available. One of the rooms he had built, on speculation, was an eighteenth-century Queen Anne–style dining room with fireplace set in a paneled wall and with architectural details typical of the period. Ruth McChesney saw it, liked it, and bought it. Since then, Richard has built many of the rooms Ruth has added to her collection.

"I would consider my professional career in miniatures in two stages," Richard explains, "pre–Mrs. McChesney and post–Mrs. McChesney. I have always tried to do the best I possibly can, but it took me a long time to learn the miniature business. It's really a matter of lengthy practice and minute observation. I'd love to do the impossible and rebuild the first room I ever made. But these recent projects are professional at every stage of development, and working with Mrs. McChesney has been a dedicated craftsman's dream come true.

"If I should get out of this business," Richard goes on, "at least I would know that I worked successfully with an exacting professional and have done the best work I could possibly do."

Richard works in a small studio with space for one room in progress at a time. The studio is filled with the same full-sized shop tools used by cabinetmakers. Unlike most artisans who build miniature rooms, every component in one of Richard's rooms is handcrafted. "When I first got into miniatures, long ago," Richard reminisces, "I decided to try to do this without ever buying any already fabricated product."

When planning a miniature room, Richard tries to gather authentic materials that are appropriate to each architectural style. For example, he searches out walnut, oak, or heart pine for floors and pine, mahogany, or oak for paneled walls, and he makes sure that the grain is the proper miniature scale.

If mixed-media faux finishes or elaborately shaped painted moldings are needed, Richard uses pattern pine. "This is the clearest of sugar pines, cut from the heart of very old trees and so carefully kiln-dried that it has virtually no shrinkage," he says. "I cut and shape all of my complex moldings from this clear pine since it keeps a sharp edge and has no tendency to warp or cup." Each project is one of a kind in that he makes all the moldings for a specific room in quantities sufficient for that room only.

Looking ahead, Richard says "I have all sorts of rooms I'd love to do, and many contexts I'd like to see them in. Each new room is a challenge to achieve precision, coupled with charm." Each room is another step in the career of a superb miniaturist who thought he might become a stage set designer one day.

# 23
# JEAN WICKWIRE

Creating plant materials and flower arrangements for a miniature room setting is one of the most difficult aspects of the project. Plants must be believable to the viewer's eye, and they must be virtually indestructible. Jean Wickwire's artistry and the medium she uses fill both requirements.

Jean found the medium she uses for flowers while crafting items with her friend June Arrott to sell through the Women's Exchange. "One of the projects we were doing," she remembers, "was making little animals out of oil cans. We needed something for the ears and we discovered this tape. You can do anything with it." Because working with tin was too difficult for her hands, Jean began thinking of other uses for the tape: "I had always been interested in flowers, and I wondered if I could do flowers with this tape, and I found that I could." The tape Jean uses is a type of duct tape used most often by plumbers and roofers and for automobile repair, she explains. "It has a sticky side, so they could clean up a hole, put this on and paint over it." The Dutch Brand division of Nashua Corporation is one of the manufacturers of the tape, which is sold in rolls in various widths and in several weights. 3M makes a similar product.

Jean also uses various gauges of wire in the course of her work. "Very

often," she points out, "I use beading wire, which is the finest grade. I also use floral tape, acrylic paint, and even aluminum foil." The final result is "indestructible," she says, as well as beautiful and as accurate as humanly possible.

Jean and Ruth had been neighbors and friends for quite some time before Jean began making flowers for Ruth's rooms. "I had been making life-sized small wildflowers," Jean comments, "because that was what interested me. I work from botanical wildflower books and try to copy them. So I was working with small flowers but nothing like this until I thought, I wonder if I could."

Jean usually begins construction of a flower by putting two pieces of the duct tape together, with a length of wire between them. Then she begins the painstaking process of cutting out each individual part and petal of the flower. "It's a long process," she relates. Her tools are an eclectic assortment. She uses tiny scissors, needle-nosed pliers, and pins to manipulate the tape into the shapes she wants. "I even asked my dentist for a couple of his instruments," she says.

"The leaves are the easiest part," Jean comments. "There are just the two pieces of tape, and the wire itself makes it look as though that is the vein." Once all the parts of the flower are shaped, they must be dipped in a solution to allow them to accept paint. Since the product she uses for this step is no longer on the market, Jean is fortunate to have a sufficient supply.

"I do not put the flower together until I have painted all the various sections," she explains. "It's much easier." After the paint has dried, each flower is assembled and the assortment is delivered to Ruth, who, with Dick Smith's help, designs the arrangements in their proper receptacles for placement in the miniature room.

Every arrangement has been researched to authenticate the flowers of the period.

"It's always a challenge to me," Jean continues, "to see if I can do a certain kind of flower. I thought I never could do a tulip, but working with this tape, I found that I could. You know, one thing leads to another, and I've always loved working with my hands." With the help of a medium she discovered by accident, Jean Wickwire has been able to make, in miniature, that tulip and any other flower she can envision.

# INDEX